Table of Contents

HIStory / 3

Introduction – Restoration / 9

Intro to 9 Movements / 19

The 9 Movements / 22

The Prophecies that Foretold and the Resurrection that Bears Witness that Christ is the One True God: An Essay for Those that Doubt / 75

Acknowledgements

I dedicate this book to Jesus Christ, because without him I would be nothing; my children because they are my everything; my family because we have all gone through transformation together; and all the wonderful people that have been a beautiful part of this journey called life, ministry and recovery. Each one of you know who you are and have all had a tremendous impact on me.

HIStory

God has an amazing ability to orchestrate every molecule in the universe to bring each individual into submission, when it is their time to enter the kingdom. That is exactly what he did with me and he made sure I was aware that it was him and that he was real. I needed to be woken up from my sleep and he knew exactly how to do it. I had been getting loaded for twenty-one years of my life and was on the streets for the last twelve of those years. I had been raised in a Christian home, but my father was an alcoholic and my mother was co-dependent. When they divorced I tried to find in the world, what I could only find in God. By the time I was thirty-one years old, I had been pregnant five times, had had a forced abortion, and three living children. They had all been taken away from me because I had been in severely abusive relationships, which I now know were a product of sexual trafficking.

The birth of my son was a result of being locked in a house by an older man and abused for months at a time. Although, my son was a huge blessing and brought the only light I had in my life at the time, I was so broken and beaten down that I just did not know how to fight, how to stand, how to be strong, how to support myself, and how to just let God love me; because I did not love myself. I finally made it out of the apartment that I was locked in for months and called 9-1-1 and he went to jail. I found another abuser and had two more children. Unfortunately, I did not know that both of my abusers knew each other and had been in jail together. By the time I found out, my children had been taken from me and my second abuser kicked me out on the streets. I was unemployed, with no education, and homeless trying to fight for them. The two fathers terrorized me on the streets and finally after two years of sitting in law libraries trying to learn the Arizona Revised Statutes in hopes of getting my kids back, my rights were severed.

    I just wanted to die. I tried to do as much dope as I could, so that I would die; but I never did. I was one of those people you see, walking the streets, dragging a bag or carrying a backpack. I would usually sleep on bus benches and even if a man would buy me a house or an apartment, I was so paranoid and distrusting of men, that I would choose to sleep on a bus bench anyway. I had a storage unit that I kept my clothes, my law books, my pictures of my kids, and my artwork in. One day I was on my face, just sobbing for my children. I cried out to God, **"If I could just hold one of my kids for 5 seconds, I would give my life."**

Shortly after, I found out I was pregnant again and could not stop the downward spiral I had allowed the enemy to catapult me into. All of sudden, my high school sweetheart from 12 years prior and across the country got a hold of me. This was before Facebook or any social media and I was off the map for those 12 years. My family even had missing persons out on me. I still have no idea how he found me. I told him how bad my life was and thought that would scare him away. He told me he would fly me to Florida to get me sober. I got on the plane 4/15/08, that is my sobriety date. Unfortunately, he was just as bad on heroin as I was on meth, but it was the first time I saw myself from the outside. He was the last person, besides my children that I cared about, and I was heartbroken. I finally realized what I had been putting my children through.

My father flew me back to Arizona and I got into a halfway house. My life began to change when I worked the program, and I learned that God loved me and wanted good for me. I finally went to the doctor and found out that the baby had Potter's Syndrome and would not live. Potter's Syndrome is when there are no kidneys and because of that, the lungs are under-developed, and the heart is three sizes too big. When I went back to the halfway house, the women surrounded me and prayed over me. Babies with Potter's Syndrome are usually stillborn or live for 1-4 hours, suffer and then die. When the doctor told me, I asked him to use the bathroom, I hit my knees and prayed and put everything in God's hands. I called my mentor and she walked me through how to cope. I worked the program with the desperation of a drowning woman. God did not cause this to happen, but he used my circumstances to light a fire within me, to humble me, to make me completely submitted to him.

The day came, when I was rushed to the hospital, full-term, they were about to cut me open because the umbilical cord was coming out. They had strapped my arms down like Jesus on the cross. I told them the baby had Potter's Syndrome. They checked for the heartbeat and there was none. It was like the world just stopped and I laid there, strapped down like Jesus. They induced labor, and the baby (Matthew Isaiah) was stillborn. They asked me if I wanted to hold him, I said yes. I held him in my arms for five seconds, it was like a flash of light, I remembered that prayer I prayed when I was homeless, "If I could just hold one of my kids for five more seconds, I would give my life. I had no idea that I would be giving my life to Jesus and that he would use it as a testimony to what he could do. I knew in that moment that he was real. He was the only person who could have heard that prayer.

I have been serving him with everything in me ever since, sharing my testimony and ministering to women just like me. It amazes me how powerful, loving, compassionate, trustworthy, and glorious that God is and always will be. I have a ministry called IdentiFreed, which means Identified by Adoption and Freed by Grace. We go out into halfway houses, shelters and churches to bring the message of freedom, deliverance and salvation to the broken and hungry. We also boost live on Facebook into over countries all over the world. My hunger for evangelism continues to grow every day. I have a beautiful daughter who is almost five and have reconciled with my oldest child, my baby boy who is now 18 years old. I have earned three degrees and am now working on Master of Divinity. My message is that God is real, and his love is enough to pull anyone back from the gates of death. Never give up, you have not gone too far for his love to reach you.

Introduction – Restoration

Restoration occurs when we truly understand our Identity in Christ. Understanding the experience and condition of walking in the flesh, and the impact that it has on inhibiting our desire to turn to God for the answer to all our problems; is the pivotal point in turning every part of our lives over to God. When we truly understand that we have been "Identified by Adoption" into the sonship with Jesus Christ and that through his work on the cross we are "Freed by Grace", a dynamic unleashing begins, and we are no longer held captive to our afflictions.

Identification

Paul talks about the condition of the flesh when he states,

"¹⁴ We know that the law is spiritual; but I am unspiritual, sold as a **slave to sin**. ¹⁵ I do not understand what I do. For what I want to do I do not do, but what I hate I do. ¹⁶ And if I do what I do not want to do, I agree that the law is good. ¹⁷ As it is, it is no longer I myself who do it, but **it is sin living in me**. ¹⁸ For I know that good itself does not dwell in me, that is, in my sinful nature.[a] For <u>I have the desire to do</u>

<u>what is good, but I cannot carry it out</u>. ¹⁹ For I do not do the good I want to do, but the evil I do not want to do—this I keep on doing. ²⁰ **<u>Now if I do what I do not want to do, it is no longer I who do it, but it is sin living in me that does it</u>**". (Romans 7:14-25 [New International Version]).

By identifying the root issue that is preventing us from being led by the spirit, achieving and maintaining intimacy with Christ, and keeps us in bondage; we are then free to step into the solution. The Big Book of Alcoholics Anonymous talks about this condition and refers to it as the physical allergy and mental obsession.[1] When I disciple my girls, I refer to it as "learning I am walking in the flesh and that need to learn how to walk in the spirit".

Surrender

"Submit yourselves, then, to God. Resist the devil, and he will flee from you." (James 4:7 [NIV]).

Once you realize that the enemy has full reign to control you through your fleshly desires, and that only God's power can overcome that, then there is only one choice. Turning to God, results

---

[1] Alcoholics Anonymous World Services, Inc., *Alcoholics Anonymous*. (New York City: The AA Grapevine, 2001), xxviii, 23, accessed February 22, 2018, http://research.easybib.com/research/index/search?search=%22Alcoholics+Anonymous%22&&sort_by=rank&medium=on_line&filters%5Bdatasource%5D=easybib

in resisting the devil. When we turn to God and accept Jesus Christ as our Lord and Savior, we have chosen to enter the kingdom of heaven manifesting on earth. We then have access to all that Jesus did when He walked the earth. Every miracle, every blessing and the strength and power to overcome every temptation the enemy may throw our way. Does that mean we will be perfect and never stumble? No, that means that we will have the greatest power in the universe working through us to counsel, guide and help us overcome everything we will ever face.

Open Heart to Receive God

It is essential to have an open heart to receive God. I have worked with hundreds of women over the past ten years and it is impossible to receive God with a hardened heart. My prayer for all those reading this book is that your hearts would be healed of all trauma you have experienced, especially through the church or any type of father figure. I pray that the Holy Spirit would pour healing oil over every emotional scar that you have ever encountered through society, that would bar you from viewing God as anything, but loving. If that is you, please do not forget to add those wounds and offenses on your inventory. We must disassociate with all earthly perceptions of God or men that have skewed our ability to receive God's love and grace openly, with no restraints and no reservations that we are unworthy of His love. It is through Christ that we are justified and worthy of God's love, forgiveness, grace and mercy.

> "The earlier revelation was intended simply to get us ready for the Messiah, who then puts everything right for those who trust him to do it. Moses wrote that anyone who insists on using the law code to live right before God soon discovers it's not so easy—every detail of life regulated by fine print! But trusting God to shape the right living in us is a different story—no precarious climb up to heaven to recruit the Messiah, no dangerous descent into hell to rescue the Messiah. So, what exactly was Moses saying?
> **The word that saves is right here,**
>   **as near as the tongue in your mouth,**
>   **as close as the heart in your chest.**
> **It's the word of faith that welcomes God to go to work and set things right for us. This is the core of our preaching. Say the welcoming word to God—*"Jesus is my Master"*—embracing, body and soul, God's work of doing in us what he did in raising Jesus from the dead. That's it. You're not "doing" anything; you're simply calling out to God, trusting him to do it for you. That's salvation. With your whole being you embrace God setting things right, and then you say it, right out loud: *"God has set everything right between him and me!"*** (Romans 10:9-10 [The Message]).

Restoration

God loves to show off and take those of us that are considered broken, by the definition of the world, and use us to show off His power and glory. It is then unmistakable to anyone, that it is purely an act of God when we are transformed. Restoration is a process. God will take the time that you have lost with Him and restore that first if you are open to allowing Him first place in your life. When we experience His unconditional love, the only choice that we have, is to chase after Him with everything in us. By focusing on Him and running after Him, afflictions melt away, our paths are changed, and He restores what is good according to His purpose. The following are verses that you should meditate on over the course of going through the 9 movements.

"As for you, you were dead in your transgressions and sins, ² in which you used to live when you followed the ways of this world and of the ruler of the kingdom of the air, the spirit who is now at work in those who are disobedient. ³ All of us also lived among them at one time, gratifying the cravings of our flesh[a] and following its desires and thoughts. Like the rest, we were by nature deserving of wrath. ⁴ But **because of his great love for us, God, who is rich in mercy, ⁵ made us alive with Christ even when we were dead in transgressions—it is by grace you have been saved**. ⁶ And God raised us up with Christ and seated us with him in the heavenly realms in Christ Jesus, ⁷ in order that in the coming ages he might show the incomparable riches of his grace, expressed in his kindness to us in Christ Jesus. ⁸ For it is by grace you have been saved, through faith—and this is not from yourselves, it is the gift of God— ⁹ not by works, so that no one can boast. ¹⁰ For we are God's handiwork, created in Christ Jesus to do good works, which God prepared in advance for us to do." (Ephesians 2 [NIV]).

"I will repay you for the years the locusts have eaten—
  the great locust and the young locust,
  the other locusts and the locust swarm[a]—
my great army that I sent among you.
²⁶ You will have plenty to eat, until you are full,
  and you will praise the name of the LORD your God,
  who has worked wonders for you;
never again will my people be shamed." (Joel 2:25-27 [NIV]).

"I am the true vine, and my Father is the gardener. ² He cuts off every branch in me that bears no fruit, while every branch that does bear fruit he prunes[a] so that it will be even more fruitful. ³ You are already clean because of the word I have spoken to you. ⁴ Remain in me, as I also remain in you. No branch can bear fruit by itself; it must remain in the vine. Neither can you bear fruit unless you remain in me.

⁵ "I am the vine; you are the branches. If you remain in me and I in you, you will bear much fruit; apart from me you can do nothing. ⁶ If you do not remain in me, you are like a branch that is thrown away and withers; such branches are picked up, thrown into the fire and burned. ⁷ If you remain in me and my words remain in you, ask whatever you wish, and it will be done for you." (John 15:1-7 [NIV]).

"Do not conform to the pattern of this world, but be transformed by the renewing of your mind. Then you will be able to test and approve what God's will is—his good, pleasing and perfect will." (Romans 12:2 [NIV]).

Definitions that are key to the journey.

RECOVER

1.

return to a normal state of health, mind, or strength.

synonyms: recuperate, get better, convalesce, regain one's

strength, get stronger, get back on one's feet.

2.

find or regain possession of (something stolen or lost).

synonyms: retrieve, **regain (possession of)**, get back, recoup, **reclaim, repossess, redeem,** recuperate, find (again), track down

MUTUALLY EXCLUSIVE

"Mutually exclusive" is a statistical term describing two or more events that cannot occur simultaneously" [2] Collectively exhaustive means that one of the events must occur.

These statistical terms are quite applicable to addiction or walking in the flesh. If one continues to feed their flesh, they will surely die; if not physically, then spiritually, that is the mutually exclusive part. They must find God, to be released from bondage, this is the collectively exhaustive component. Basically, find God or die.

Well, that is a tough pill for those carrying offense against God to carry. That is why we have all these different programs that people have created to try to remove the God element out of recovery. Well, that is just what it is, a body of people continually recovering, but none recovered. When we continue to try another way, feeding the flesh will manifest in some other way.

---

[2] Investopedia. *Mututally Exclusive.* Investopedia.com
https://www.investopedia.com/terms/m/mutuallyexclusive.asp

IdentiFreed

Intro to 9 Movements

In Romans 12:2 it says that, "we will be transformed by the renewing of our minds. If I have an old computer program that is not compatible with my current software, I need to upgrade. Getting sober and not going through deliverance is like trying to play an 8 track on an iPhone. Being RECOVERED is about destroying files to make room for new ones. Being TRANSFORMED means running an entirely new operating system. Are you ready for the download?

If you are currently working a program, this will just be an extension of what you already know, and you will have so much more to offer on a completely different level. Keep an open mind. There are many in the church that believe that the 12 steps are not in line with what we believe, however, they just teach us how to live out the Christian principles. The 9 movements are an adapted version of the steps that may be more palpable to the believer. Do not stop working your program or going to meetings and do not feel disheartened when those in the church do not understand the necessity for spiritual growth. Just be the light in the rooms and walk in humility and forgiveness toward those that do not understand. Those of us that have struggled in the flesh, must seek constant spiritual growth. God showed me that nine instead of twelve and then I discovered that nine means the perfect movement of God.

9 The Perfect Movement of God

> "Used 49 times in Scripture, the number 9 symbolizes divine completeness or conveys the meaning of finality. Christ died at the 9th hour of the day, or 3 p.m., to make the way of salvation open to everyone. The Day of Atonement (Yom Kippur) is the only one of God's annual Feast days of worship that requires believers to fast for one day. This special day, considered by many Jews to be the holiest of the year, begins at sunset on the 9th day of the seventh Hebrew month (Leviticus 23:32).
>
> Nine also represents the fruits of God's Holy Spirit, which are Faithfulness, Gentleness, Goodness, Joy, Kindness, Long suffering, Love, Peace and Self-control (Galatians 5:22 - 23).
>
> ***Appearances of the number nine***
>
> In was at the 9th hour of the day that a Roman Centurion named Cornelius was told, in a vision, to contact the apostle Peter. Cornelius would eventually be baptized and receive God's spirit, becoming the first recorded Gentile convert to Christianity (Acts 10)." [3]

The 9 Movements

1. We discover that we are walking in the flesh and need to learn how to walk in the Spirit.

The first movement is discovering that we are trying to solve all our problems by feeding our flesh. It is the manifestation of an effort to attempt to control the chaos in this fallen world by feeding the flesh. Paul explains this battle of flesh perfectly,

> "For I know that good itself does not dwell in me, that is, in my sinful nature.[a] For I have the desire to do what is good, but I cannot carry it out. 19 For I do not do the good I want to do, but the evil I do not want to do—this I keep on doing. 20 Now if I do what I do not want to do, it is no longer I who do it, but it is sin living in me that does it." (Romans 7:18-20 [NIV]).

No matter how badly we do not want to feed our flesh, we continue to do so until the physical cycle is broken. Often, this must occur through detox or fasting the addictive or repetitive behavior. However, even when that cycle is broken; in fact, especially when it is broken, the enemy will try to come in and tempt. He tempted

---

[3] The Bible Study Site. *Meaning of Numbers in the Bible the Number 9*. Biblestudy.org

http://www.biblestudy.org/bibleref/meaning-of-numbers-in-bible/9.html

Jesus, of course he is going to tempt those that choose to follow him. Part of learning how to walk in the spirit is learning how to deflect the fiery darts of the enemy (Eph 6:10-18) and to allow the Holy Spirit to raise up a standard and lead us. (Isaiah 59:19) That is what going through the rest of the movements are about. Each one brings you closer into learning how to walk in the spirit.

Results of Learning How to Walk in The Spirit

"I am the vine; you are the branches. If you remain in me and I in you, you will bear much fruit; apart from me you can do nothing." (John 15:5 [NIV]).

Once we learn how to resist the devil by not submitting to our fleshly desires, we then allow the Holy Spirit to lead us into every action. The Message version says it this way,

> 5-8 "I am the Vine, you are the branches. When you're joined with me and I with you, the relation intimate and organic, the harvest is sure to be abundant. Separated, you can't produce a thing. Anyone who separates from me is deadwood, gathered up and thrown on the bonfire. But if you make yourselves at home with me and my words are at home in you, you can be sure that whatever you ask will be listened to and acted upon. This is how my Father shows who he is—when you produce grapes, when you mature as my disciples." (John 15:5-8 [MSG]).

Write down how you have been walking in the flesh (examples: addiction of any kind, self-righteousness, fear, anxiety, co-dependence, etc.):

_____
_____
_____
_____
_____
_____
_____
_____
_____
_____
_____
_____
_____
_____
_____
_____

2. We believe that Jesus Christ is the Messiah and that His finished work on the cross defeated sickness and death and has given us access to the same resurrection power to overcome our afflictions.

Believing that Jesus Christ is the one true God and came in the form of a man is difficult for people to digest. Therefore, there are so many people trying to seek another way. God is about an experience. If you are struggling with the belief in Jesus Christ as Lord and savior, please pray for him to reveal himself to you and read the essay at the back of this book, "The Prophecies that Foretold and the Resurrection that Bears Witness that Christ is the One True God: An Essay for Those that Doubt".

For those that already believe, you may have had the experience where you have given your heart to Christ, yet you continue to struggle with the flesh. Please stop beating yourself up and allowing the enemy full reign to do the same. The whole reason that Jesus died on the cross was to take all our afflictions on him. Does this mean to continue sinning? No, but once we have submitted to a chronic sin in our lives it is difficult to overcome the flesh. It is only by the resurrection power of Christ that the horrendous cycle can be broken. We may be strong believers but have not encountered the power of the Holy Spirit. Or we may believe fully in the power but feel so downtrodden that we don't believe his healing power applies to a specific issue. That is a lie from the enemy. We must believe with every cell in our body that the healing power of Jesus Christ, will deliver us from every affliction.

Verses about the resurrection power of Christ.

"But he was pierced for our transgressions, he was crushed for our iniquities; the punishment that brought us peace was on him, and by his wounds we are healed." (Isaiah 53:5 [NIV]).

"He himself bore our sins" in his body on the cross, so that we might die to sins and live for righteousness; "by his wounds you have been healed." (1 Peter 2:24 [NIV]).

"God made him who had no sin to be sin[a] for us, so that in him we might become the righteousness of God." (2 Corinthians 5:21 [NIV]).

"For the Spirit God gave us does not make us timid, but give us power, love and self-discipline" (2 Timothy 1:7 [NIV]).

This means that we will rest in his love and power and trust that he will give us peace and guide us on this journey. Regardless of what we face, we begin to rest in his power and peace and trust that he will work everything out for our good. When we truly understand the power of the living God, the resurrected king, then we unlock our identity in Christ and learn to walk in complete freedom…IdentiFreed: Identified by Adoption and Freed by Grace.

"And we know that in all things God works for the good of those who love him, who have been called according to his purpose." (Romans 8:28 [NIV]).

Stories of Healing in the Bible.

There are so many people that Jesus healed during his ministry. Studying these encounters allows the same miracle to then activate in our lives. That is why sharing our testimonies is so powerful. Once we hear that another person has experienced a miraculous healing, we then believe that it is possible for us too. The woman with the blood born illness suffered for twelve years and then finally came into the presence of Jesus and reached out to touch him, it is then that she was healed.

> "43 And a woman was there who had been subject to bleeding for twelve years, but no one could heal her. 44 She came up behind him and touched the edge of his cloak, and immediately her bleeding stopped.
>
> 45 "Who touched me?" Jesus asked.
>
> When they all denied it, Peter said, "Master, the people are crowding and pressing against you."
>
> 46 But Jesus said, "Someone touched me; I know that power has gone out from me."
>
> 47 Then the woman, seeing that she could not go unnoticed, came trembling and fell at his feet. In the presence of all the people, she told why she had touched him and how she had been instantly healed. 48 Then he said to her, '**Daughter, your faith has healed you. Go in peace.**'" (Luke 8:43-48 [NIV]).

It is our faith that ignites the extent of healing that is available to us. Sometimes people just don't believe God can heal, then there are some that believe that God can heal, but that he will not heal them because of limitations they have placed on God or even themselves because of their sin. That is why it is so important to go through the rest of the movements. Right now, all you have to do is to believe that God can heal and deliver you and trust that he will.

The other side of this experience is when people encounter the healing power of the Holy Spirit and refuse to acknowledge God for their healing. We see this all the time in the rooms of recovery. When we experience deliverance, we must give glory to God and recognize that the miracle has happened. We no longer need to declare the affliction over us, but freedom from the same. The story of the lepers is the perfect example,

> "11 Now on his way to Jerusalem, Jesus traveled along the border between Samaria and Galilee. 12 As he was going into a village, ten men who had leprosy met him. They stood at a distance 13 and called out in a loud voice, "Jesus, Master, have pity on us!"
>
> 14 When he saw them, he said, "Go, show yourselves to the priests." And as they went, they were cleansed.
>
> 15 **One of them, when he saw he was healed, came back, praising God in a loud voice. 16 He threw himself at Jesus' feet and thanked him**—and he was a Samaritan.
>
> 17 Jesus asked, "Were not all ten cleansed? Where are the other nine? 18 Has no one returned to give praise to God except this foreigner?" 19 Then he said to him, "Rise and go; **your faith has made you well.**" (Luke 17:11-19 [NIV]).

This leper was not just healed but made well. The beautiful part of the second movement is that as believers our perception of God is continually growing as we encounter him through an intimacy that is only experienced by allowing him to operate in and through us. As he continues to transform us and those that we minister to, we get to experience a multitude of miracles. No matter what denomination of Christianity you are, do not put limitations on God by the perceptions that you were raised with.

Take some time to write down your perception of God as a child:

_____

_____

_____

_____

_____

How did your perception of God change as you began to become dependent upon feeding your flesh?

_____

_____

_____

How has your perception of God changed because of your life experiences (include influences of others)?

How do you view God today?

It is extremely important to list any of the hurts associated with your perception of God in the third movement.

Deciding to be led by the Spirit.

Once we truly believe that Jesus was the Messiah and truly was crucified for the sins of the world and raised from the dead; we begin to understand the power that is available to us. When we accept him into our hearts and choose to follow him; the next move, is to ask the Holy Spirit to fill us and lead and guide us daily.

"If you declare with your mouth, "Jesus is Lord," and believe in your heart that God raised him from the dead, you will be saved. [10] For it is with your heart that you believe and are justified, and it is with your mouth that you profess your faith and are saved." (Romans 10:9-10 [NIV]).

"I will give you a new heart and put a new spirit in you; I will remove from you your heart of stone and give you a heart of flesh." (Ezekiel 36:26 [NIV]).

"Create in me a pure heart, O God, and renew a steadfast spirit within me." (Psalm 51:10 [NIV]).

> "Therefore, there is now no condemnation for those who are in Christ Jesus, ² because through Christ Jesus the law of the Spirit who gives life has set you free from the law of sin and death. ³ For what the law was powerless to do because it was weakened by the flesh, God did by sending his own Son in the likeness of sinful flesh to be a sin offering. And so he condemned sin in the flesh, ⁴ in order that the righteous requirement of the law might be fully met in us, who do not live according to the flesh but according to the Spirit.
> ⁵ Those who live according to the flesh have their minds set on what the flesh desires; but those who live in accordance with the Spirit have their minds set on what the Spirit desires. ⁶ The mind governed by the flesh is death, but the mind governed by the Spirit is life and peace. ⁷ The mind governed by the flesh is hostile to God; it does not submit to God's law, nor can it do so. ⁸ Those who are in the realm of the flesh cannot please God.
> ⁹ You, however, are not in the realm of the flesh but are in the realm of the Spirit, if indeed the Spirit of God lives in you. And if anyone does not have the Spirit of Christ, they do not belong to Christ. ¹⁰ But if Christ is in you, then even though your body is subject to death because of sin, the Spirit gives life because of righteousness. ¹¹ And if the Spirit of him who raised Jesus from the dead is living in you, he who raised Christ from the dead will also give life to your mortal bodies because of his Spirit who lives in you.
> ¹² Therefore, brothers and sisters, we have an obligation—but it is not to the flesh, to live according to it. ¹³ For if you live according to the flesh, you will die; but if by the Spirit you put to death the misdeeds of the body, you will live.
> ¹⁴ For those who are led by the Spirit of God are the children of God. ¹⁵ The Spirit you received does not make you slaves, so that you live in fear again; rather, the Spirit you received brought about your adoption to sonship. And by him we cry, *"Abba,* Father." ¹⁶ The Spirit himself testifies with our

spirit that we are God's children. ¹⁷ Now if we are children, then we are heirs—heirs of God and co-heirs with Christ, if indeed we share in his sufferings in order that we may also share in his glory." (Romans 8:1-17 [NIV]).

3. We learn to put on the full Armor of God.

"Finally, be strong in the Lord and in his mighty power. [11] Put on the full armor of God, so that you can take your stand against the devil's schemes. [12] For our struggle is not against flesh and blood, but against the rulers, against the authorities, against the powers of this dark world and against the spiritual forces of evil in the heavenly realms. [13] Therefore put on the full armor of God, so that when the day of evil comes, you may be able to stand your ground, and after you have done everything, to stand. [14] Stand firm then, with the belt of truth buckled around your waist, with the breastplate of righteousness in place, [15] and with your feet fitted with the readiness that comes from the gospel of peace. [16] In addition to all this, take up the shield of faith, with which you can extinguish all the flaming arrows of the evil one. [17] Take the helmet of salvation and the sword of the Spirit, which is the word of God." (Eph 6:10-18 [NIV]).

The most important part of deliverance is truly learning how to put on the full armor of God by completing an assessment of all animosity, fear and relationship behaviors. I have worked with hundreds of women and those that were raised in the church may say, "I forgive everyone and hold no resentments". Just because we are taught to forgive, does not mean that we did not experience the resentment and process it in an unhealthy way. If we are taught to never process through how we feel, we often manifest unhealthy and dysfunctional patterns. Please be open to this exercise, the more work you put in the more freedom you will experience.

To be totally delivered from the bondage of the flesh, we must be free of all traumatic and hurtful events that have created soul wounds which allow the enemy to be able penetrate the chink in our armor or manipulate us through our weak spot. We must seal up our armor by being completely thorough and taking this journey with a mentor that is a believer.

The first part of the life assessment is writing down all offenses that you have experienced in your entire life. Start at the beginning and go through in chronological order. This will help your mentor to see the areas that you have experienced trauma. Mentors, if your mentee has a large gap in their life that they cannot remember and begin recalling at a specific time period other than childhood, this will show you where the trauma has occurred. You will need to pray for the Holy Spirit to guide and heal and may need to write these out with your mentee.

Conversely, if you who are in the assessment process cannot remember, just ask the Holy Spirit to reveal to you what you are supposed to see. In the first column list the person or concept that caused the offense or created animosity and in the second column list the offense. Leave the third column blank and start praying for the person or concept that you hold offense against. Move on to the next offense and go through your entire life. It works best to put the first two column on the left side of an open notebook and the third column on the right side. Or just use an excel spreadsheet if possible.

Column 1	Column 2	Column 3
Name or Concept	Offense	Processing Analysis (leave blank for now)

After you have written all the hurts throughout your entire life, truly pray for all the people on the list. Include animosity that you are holding against yourself. Just put one offense per section. Do not list all offenses against that one person in one section.

Miracles take place in the spiritual when we unleash forgiveness.

This assessment is not about condemnation, it is a roadmap to teach you how to release forgiveness, pray for soul wounds, and become a warrior in learning how to put on the Full Armor of God.

Just reading the verse every day, will not teach you how to walk out the concepts found in that beautiful verse.

"For if you forgive other people when they sin against you, your heavenly Father will also forgive you. ¹⁵ But if you do not forgive others their sins, your Father will not forgive your sins." (Matthew 6:14-15 [NIV]).

> "he does not treat us as our sins deserve or repay us according to our iniquities. ¹¹ For as high as the heavens are above the earth, so great is his love for those who fear him; ¹² as far as the east is from the west, so far has he removed our transgressions from us.
> ¹³ As a father has compassion on his children, so the LORD has compassion on those who fear him; ¹⁴ for he knows how we are formed, he remembers that we are dust." (Psalm 103:14-15 [NIV]).

"Then Peter came up and said to him, "Lord, how often will my brother sin against me, and I forgive him? As many as seven times?" Jesus said to him, "I do not say to you seven times, but seventy times seven." (Matthew 18:21-22 [ESV]).

"Be kind to one another, tenderhearted, forgiving one another, as God in Christ forgave you." (Ephesians 4:32 [ESV]).

Column 3 – Unforgiveness is a stronghold.

A stronghold is defined as a place that has been fortified to protect against attack. Another definition is a place where a particular cause or belief is strongly defended or upheld. When we experience trauma, we have a specified reaction that is often grounded in delusion to deal with reality. The more often that we react with the same perspective, we strengthen the neuropathway that was created when we first perceived the situation in a specific way. To compound the issue, we respond in a way that feeds our flesh with self-seeking behavior. To analyze this and ask God to heal it, we need to proceed to the third column. We have already listed column 1 and 2.

In the third column we will not look at the offense, but only how we processed and responded to it. We will write how our behavior or thought patterns were "selfish, dishonest, and self-seeking", we will list the "fear" that was driving us and where we were "to blame", please write what the healthy alternative would have been regarding how you processed the hurt. All of these are taken directly from the 4th column of the AA inventory with a slight difference in the "to blame" section. [4] The most important thing that I teach my girls is that the dishonesty is not always outward dishonesty, often it manifests as inward dishonesty or delusion. Think about it, a child that grows up in a dysfunctional home with an addict or alcoholic may have experienced empty promises of change from the afflicted person. This continual cycle of living in expectation of change teaches the child to live in delusion. In fact, believing one thing and seeing something totally different becomes second nature. This delusional state of existence teaches one to enjoy the world of imagination, much more than reality. That is why substances or feeding the flesh create an escape that consists of little energy or thought and is somewhat of a relief requiring limited effort, comparatively speaking.

The following are what I refer to with my girls as the Fab 7 (for my early mentees, what we used to call the Fab 5:

---

[4] Alcoholics Anonymous World Services, Inc., *Alcoholics Anonymous*. (New York City: The AA Grapevine, 2001) 67, accessed February 22, 2018,

http://research.easybib.com/research/index/search?search=%22Alcoholics+Anonymous%22&&sort_by=rank&medium=on_line&filters%5Bdatasource%5D=easybib

- Not expressing feelings or ideas
- Hiding reality–not facing facts
- Stubbornly holding on to inaccurate beliefs
- Lying to myself
- Exaggerating, minimalizing
- Setting myself up to be "wronged"
- Expecting others to be what they are not

As believers we do not walk in condemnation, but it is important for us to look at what reactions we had that were inappropriate or unhealthy and how we can respond in a more Christlike and healthy manner. The best way to tear down a stronghold or embedded neuropathway is to create a new one, that is why the last part of the third column, "healthy alternative" creates a roadmap of how to deal with the same situation in a healthier way. Essentially, this process will assist us in the renewing or transformation of our mind and unhealthy dysfunctional patterns.

IdentiFreed

Column 1	Column 2	Column 3
Name	Offense	Stronghold
Person or concept	1st event	Selfish: Dishonest: Self-Seeking: Fear: To Blame (healthy alternative):
Person or concept	2nd event	Selfish: Dishonest: Self-Seeking: Fear: To Blame (healthy alternative):

IdentiFreed

"SELFISH
- Not seeing others point of view, problems or needs
- Wanting things my way
- Wanting special treatment
- Wanting others to meet my needs–dependence
- Wanting what others have
- Wanting to control–dominance
- Thinking I'm better–grandiosity
- Wanting to be the best
- Thinking others are jealous
- Wanting others to be like me
- Being miserly, possessive
- Wanting more than my share
- Reacting from self-loathing, self righteousness
- Too concerned about me
- Not trying to be a friend
- Wanting to look good or be liked
- Concerned only with my needs

DISHONEST
- Not seeing or admitting where I was at fault
- Having a superior attitude–thinking I'm better
- Blaming others for my problems
- Not admitting I've done the same thing
- Not expressing feelings or ideas
- Not being clear about motives
- Lying, cheating, stealing
- Hiding reality–not facing facts
- Stubbornly holding on to inaccurate beliefs
- Breaking rules
- Lying to myself
- Exaggerating, minimalizing
- Setting myself up to be "wronged"
- Expecting others to be what they are not
- Being perfectionistic

SELF-SEEKING
- Manipulating others to do my will
- Putting others down internally or externally to build me up
- Engaging in character assassination
- Acting superior
- Acting to fill a void
- Engaging in gluttony or lusting at the expense of another person
- Ignoring others' needs
- Trying to control others

- Getting revenge when I don't get what I want
- Holding a resentment
- Acting to make me feel good

FRIGHTENED (OF)

- Peoples' opinions

- Rejection, abandonment
- Loneliness
- Physical injury, abuse
- Not being able to control or change someone
- My inferiority, inadequacy
- Criticism
- Expressing ideas or feelings
- Getting trapped
- Exposure, embarrassment"

---

[5] Overeaters Anonymous. *Step Four Resentments Checklist Column 4.* Oapalmbeachfl.org

http://oapalmbeachfl.org/documents/Step4_Inventory_Sheets.pdf

"For the weapons of our warfare are not of the flesh but have divine power to <u>destroy strongholds</u>." (2 Corinthians 10:4 [ESV]).

"Do not be conformed to this world, but be transformed by the renewal of your mind, that by testing you may discern what is the will of God, what is good and acceptable and perfect." (Romans 12:2 [ESV]).

> "Finally, be strong in the Lord and in his mighty power. [11] Put on the full armor of God, so that you can take your stand against the devil's schemes. [12] For our struggle is not against flesh and blood, but against the rulers, against the authorities, against the powers of this dark world and against the spiritual forces of evil in the heavenly realms.[13] Therefore put on the full armor of God, so that when the day of evil comes, you may be able to stand your ground, and after you have done everything, to stand. [14] Stand firm then, with the belt of truth buckled around your waist, with the breastplate of righteousness in place, [15] and with your feet fitted with the readiness that comes from the gospel of peace. [16] In addition to all this, take up the shield of faith, with which you can extinguish all the flaming arrows of the evil one. [17] Take the helmet of salvation and the sword of the Spirit, which is the word of God.
>
> [18] And pray in the Spirit on all occasions with all kinds of prayers and requests. With this in mind, be alert and always

keep on praying for all the Lord's people." (Ephesians 6:10-18 [NIV]).

"For though we walk in the flesh, we are not waging war according to the flesh. For the weapons of our warfare are not of the flesh but have divine power to destroy strongholds. We destroy arguments and every lofty opinion raised against the knowledge of God, and take every thought captive to obey Christ" (2 Corinthians 10:3-5 [ESV]).

Forgiveness Definitions

> Dictionary: to stop blaming or being angry with someone for something they have done, or not punish them for something. The pardon of an offender, by which he is considered and treated as not guilty.

> The various Hebrew words for forgiveness stress the idea of wiping out or blotting out the memory of the sin, covering or concealing the record of the sin, lifting up and removal of sin, passing by of sin, and pardoning on the basis of a substitute

Salach: to forgive or pardon

Kapar: atonement, removal of sin or defilement

Nasa: to lift up, to carry or support, to take up or away

Greek: release, as from bondage, imprisonment, forgiveness, pardon, of sins; the process of setting free or liberating. Forgiveness, pardon, of sins (properly, the letting them go, as if they had not been committed.

Charizomai: to be gracious, to give freely, canceling a debt

Aphiemi: to dismiss the crime or resentment, release the person

Aphesis: remission of sin, freedom and release

God's Forgiveness: Only God can cover, remove, pardon and forgive sin on the basis of Christ's shed blood.

Relationship History

Like the previous assessment, please write about every person that you have had romantic involvement with.

You will begin writing at the beginning of life, the first relationship ever, to the most recent. This is also taken from the book of Alcoholics Anonymous because it works.

> "We reviewed our own conduct over the years past. Where had we been selfish, dishonest, or inconsiderate? Whom had we hurt? Did we unjustifiably arouse jealousy, suspicion, or bitterness? Where were we at fault, what should we have done instead? We got this all down on paper and looked at it."[6]

Name:	Selfish:
	Dishonest:
	Inconsiderate:
	Whom had I hurt:
	Jealousy:
	Suspicion:
	Bitterness:
	At Fault:
	Done Instead:

---

[6] Alcoholics Anonymous World Services, Inc., *Alcoholics Anonymous.*)New York City: The AA Grapevine, 2001) 69, accessed, February 23, 2018, http://research.easybib.com/research/index/search?search=%22Alcoholics+Anonymous%22&&sort_by=rank&medium=on_line&filters%5Bdatasource%5D=easybib

Again, this is not to shame, but to look at the pattern or strongholds that have been erected in our lives. This will also assist us in praying to break unhealthy soul ties associated with these relationships. "Hatred stirs up conflict, but love covers all wrongs." (Prov 10:12 [NIV]).

One of the important factors to recognize when we are writing this assessment is that it is not to shame or condemn, merely to become warriors against the tactics of the enemy. He usually comes through offense and fear. When we go into the next movement, we realize that all these strongholds have been rooted in reactions that arise out of fear and offense. As Pastor Michael Maiden always says, "once we reveal, God can heal it".

4. Revealing our life assessment to our mentor and praying for the Holy Spirit to heal and deliver us.

This is so important to go through the assessment with someone that you can trust. Someone that will not talk about your stuff to other people or judge you. None of us carry a superior sin to the other, we are all unworthy without Jesus. The word says that where two or more are gathered, that God is with us (Matt 18:20 [NIV]) and that what we ask in his name shall be done (John 14:13 [NIV]). This is a great exercise in learning to intercede for others, discerning spirits and counselling.

"Therefore confess your sins to each other and pray for each other so that you may be healed. The prayer of a righteous person is powerful and effective." (James 5:16 [NIV]).

"As iron sharpens iron, so one person sharpens another." (Prov 27:17 [NIV]).

As you go through the assessment together, it is important to notice when there are gaps in the memories of your life. When this happens, it is usually the brain protecting itself from trauma. A spirit led mentor should be able to recognize this and lead you into exploring what occurred and seeking God's healing. Usually, one offense or memory will lead to others that are the root offense. It is up to the mentor to be able to see these and in essence pull them from the mentee. This is why it is important to go through this with someone else, so that they can see the truth, when you are unable to.

Deliverance is being freed from the deception of the enemy. It is time to be completely set free. (See Day 28, Tearing Down Strongholds).

> "For though we live in the world, we do not wage war as the world does. 4 The weapons we fight with are not the weapons of the world. On the contrary, they have divine power to demolish strongholds. 5 We demolish arguments and every pretension that sets itself up against the knowledge of God, and we take captive every thought to make it obedient to Christ." (2 Cor 10:3-5 [NIV]).

5. Allow the Holy Spirit to lead us into healthy patterns and transform us.

After the revelation and healing that comes in the fourth movement, we see so much that we no longer want to walk in. Make a conscious choice to allow the Holy Spirit to strip you of the unhealthy behaviors that exist because of how you have processed pain and trauma in your life. Now that you have seen the ways that the enemy has come at you throughout your life, it is easy to see the fiery darts long before they are headed your way. This is where we begin to truly understand what it means to wear the full armor of God. However, it states that they will be extinguished by the faith that we have now built strong by going through the first four movements. All the actions that we have taken up to this point have been, in effect, reprogramming us to learn how to walk in the kingdom and allow the Holy Spirit in.

This is just the beginning, get in your word every day, change what you are watching and listening to and only allow in the light. Speak life over yourself, your family, your finances and your future. When you do fall into an old pattern, do not condemn yourself, just ask the Holy Spirit to lead you in the right direction. Here are some great verses to meditate on:

"A Future in God [13-16] So roll up your sleeves, put your mind in gear, be totally ready to receive the gift that's coming when Jesus arrives. Don't lazily slip back into those old grooves of evil, doing just what you feel like doing. You didn't know any better then; you do now. As obedient children, let yourselves be pulled into a way of life shaped by God's life, a life energetic and blazing with holiness. God said, "I am holy; you be holy." (1 Peter 1:13-16 [MSG]).

"To Love, to Be Loved [17-18] God is love. When we take up permanent residence in a life of love, we live in God and God lives in us. This way, love has the run of the house, becomes at home and mature in us, so that we're free of worry on Judgment Day—our standing in the world is identical with Christ's. There is no room in love for fear. Well-formed love banishes fear. Since fear is crippling, a fearful life—fear of death, fear of judgment—is one not yet fully formed in love." (1 John 4:18 [MSG]).

"Place Your Life Before God [1-2] So here's what I want you to do, God helping you: Take your everyday, ordinary life—your sleeping, eating, going-to-work, and walking-around life—and place it before God as an offering. Embracing what God does for you is the best thing you can do for him. Don't become so well-adjusted to your culture that you fit into it without even thinking. Instead, fix your attention on God. You'll be changed from the inside out. Readily recognize what he wants from you, and quickly respond to it. Unlike the culture around you, always dragging you down to its level of immaturity, God brings the best out of you, develops well-formed maturity in you." (Romans 12:2 [MSG]).

"Because of this decision we don't evaluate people by what they have or how they look. We looked at the Messiah that way once and got it all wrong, as you know. We certainly don't look at him that way anymore. Now we look inside, and what we see is that anyone united with the Messiah gets a fresh start, is created new. The old life is gone; a new life burgeons! Look at it! All this comes from the God who settled the relationship between us and him, and then called us to settle our relationships with each other. God put the world square with himself through the Messiah, giving the world a fresh start by offering forgiveness of sins. God has given us the task of telling everyone what he is doing. We're Christ's representatives. God uses us to persuade men and women to drop their differences and enter into God's work of making things right between them. We're speaking for Christ himself now: Become friends with God; he's already a friend with you." (2 Cor 5:17-20 [MSG]).

"Whenever, though, they turn to face God as Moses did, God removes the veil and there they are—face-to-face! They suddenly recognize that God is a living, personal presence, not a piece of chiseled stone. And when God is personally present, a living Spirit, that old, constricting legislation is recognized as obsolete. We're free of it! All of us! Nothing between us and God, our faces shining with the brightness of his face. And so we are transfigured much like the Messiah, our lives gradually becoming brighter and more beautiful as God enters our lives and we become like him. (2 Cor 3:18 [MSG]).

6. We seek reconciliation and restoration in all areas of our lives.

"If I speak in the tongues of men or of angels, but do not have love, I am only a resounding gong or a clanging cymbal. ² If I have the gift of prophecy and can fathom all mysteries and all knowledge, and if I have a faith that can move mountains, but do not have love, I am nothing. ³ If I give all I possess to the poor and give over my body to hardship that I may boast, but do not have love, I gain nothing.

⁴ Love is patient, love is kind. It does not envy, it does not boast, it is not proud. ⁵ It does not dishonor others, it is not self-seeking, it is not easily angered, it keeps no record of wrongs. ⁶ Love does not delight in evil but rejoices with the truth. ⁷ It always protects, always trusts, always hopes, always perseveres.

⁸ Love never fails. But where there are prophecies, they will cease; where there are tongues, they will be stilled; where there is knowledge, it will pass away. ⁹ For we know in part and we prophesy in part, ¹⁰ but when completeness comes, what is in part disappears. ¹¹ When I was a child, I talked like a child, I thought like a child, I reasoned like a child. When I became a man, I put the ways of childhood behind me. ¹² For now we see only a reflection as in a mirror; then we shall see face to face. Now I know in part; then I shall know fully, even as I am fully known.

¹³ And now these three remain: faith, hope and love. But the greatest of these is love." (1 Cor 13 [NIV]).

"Therefore if you bring your gift to the altar, and there remember that your brother has something against you, ²⁴ leave your gift there before the altar, and go your way. First be reconciled to your brother, and then come and offer your gift." (Matthew 5:23-24 [NIV]).

The sixth movement is about changing our behavior by going out and seeking reconciliation with those that we have hurt. After we have walked through the previous movements we will realize that we could have acted differently in many situations. How often have we caused harm or harbored offense and just cut off a relationship or lashed out and hurt someone. It is time to go back to each one of those people and reconcile. Yes, we are already forgiven through the power of Jesus Christ. This is not about earning our place with God, this is about caring about the healing of others as well as ourselves. When seek reconciliation and restoration in every area of our lives, God steps in and does the rest. "I will repay you for the years the locusts have eaten" (Joel 2:25 [NIV]).

Not all situations are ones that require us to do so, please go over this with your mentor. The reconciliation list should include financial, spiritual, emotional and physical damages that we have caused to others and ourselves.

Take some time to write a list of all those that you have caused financial, spiritual, emotional and physical damages to.

_____

_____

_____

_____

_____

_____

_____

_____

_____

_____

Financial reparations involve reaching out and offering to set up a payment plan. Most often we fear dealing with a financial debt because we are overwhelmed at the propensity. Most people will accept a payment plan and be grateful for the same.

Write a list of all your debts:

_____

_____

_____

_____

_____

_____

_____

_____

_____

The spiritual, emotional and physical damages caused to others and self should be written out for each person and assessed with your mentor to ensure that you are not writing with any hint of offense. Offer the individual that you are seeking restoration with the opportunity to receive it in whichever format is most palpable to them: phone, letter or in person. A great format that was used by Paul F. is listed below:

> "FACE TO FACE AMENDS
> Gain consent -
> "'I have some amends to make to you, are you open to hearing them?"
> If contacting them by phone- Ask if they would like to receive the amends on the phone, in writing, or in person.
>
> Name the wrong-
> "I was wrong when I. ...
> "I am truly sorry. You did not deserve to be treated that way.'"
>
> Ask about other harms -
> "Is there anything else I've done that has caused you harm?"
>
> Ask what you can do to right the wrong -
> "What can I do to right these wrongs?"
> Be willing to follow through on the requests. Exceptions would be to place yourself in
> danger or go against your values (theft, sex, dishonesty, deceit).
>
> Amends Letter

Dear ---
I'm writing this letter to make amends for the harm I caused you. I was wrong when I. ..
I am truly sorry. You did not deserve to be treated this way. Please let me know what I can do to
right these wrongs with you. Also let me know if there are other ways I have harmed you."

"Use your heads as you live and work among outsiders. Don't miss a trick. Make the most of every opportunity. Be gracious in your speech. The goal is to bring out the best in others in a conversation, not put them down, not cut them out." (Col 4:5-6 [MSG]).
"And the Lord's servant must not be quarrelsome but must be kind to everyone, able to teach, not resentful. 25 Opponents must be gently instructed, in the hope that God will grant them repentance leading them to a knowledge of the truth, 26 and that they will come to their senses and escape from the trap of the devil, who has taken them captive to do his will." (2 Timothy 2:24 [NIV]).

"Therefore, as God's chosen people, holy and dearly loved, clothe yourselves with compassion, kindness, humility, gentleness and patience. 13 Bear with each other and forgive one another if any of you has a grievance against someone. Forgive as the Lord forgave you." (Col 3:12-13 [NIV]).

"Blessed are the peacemakers, for they will be called children of God." (Matt 5:9 [NIV]).

When we choose to allow the Holy Spirit to work in our lives and take the action to seek restoration and reconciliation in our lives all kinds of miracles take place. Most of this will occur in our daily lives and how each day as we learn to walk in the spirit, our entire lifestyle and the way that we live and behave will change. We begin to walk in love to those around us and even to ourselves. What seemed impossible will come to pass.

> "For this reason I kneel before the Father, 15 from whom every family[a] in heaven and on earth derives its name. 16 I pray that out of his glorious riches he may strengthen you with power through his Spirit in your inner being, 17 so that Christ may dwell in your hearts through faith. And I pray that you, being rooted and established in love, 18 may have power, together with all the Lord's holy people, to grasp how wide and long and high and deep is the love of Christ, 19 and to know this love that surpasses knowledge—that you may be filled to the measure of all the fullness of God.
>
> 20 Now to him who is able to do immeasurably more than all we ask or imagine, according to his power that is at work within us," (Eph 3:14-20 [NIV]).

7. We continue to seek transformation and reconciliation through the guidance of the Holy Spirit.

This movement is the essence of walking out movements 1 through 6 daily. We stay connected with our mentor, recovery fellowships, and the church. We seek reconciliation if we react from the flesh. As we learn how to walk in the spirit, we may find that we may stumble and walk in the flesh, if we find ourselves in situations where we are continually reacting this way, we may need to make some changes and set some healthy boundaries. Continue to ask God for direction and guidance and establish a support system of at least 4 trusted people of the same sex that you can reach out to. Iron sharpens iron (Prov. 27:17).

Each day ask yourself:

1. Have I talked to God?
2. Have I meditated on the word?
3. Have I listened to God?
4. Have I been loving to others?
5. Am I concerned with my own self-interest or building up and discipling others?
6. How could I have shown God's love more purely?
7. What vision has God given me and what I have done today to work toward walking that out?
8. Was I obedient with the gifts that he has given me? How did I use them to help others today?

8. We maintain an intimacy with God through the meditating word, worship, prayer, and walk in the gifts of the spirit.

This is one of the most important movements in the process as we continue to grow in our relationship with Christ and truly hear from the Holy Spirit. We must read our **word** to understand God's heart, his promises, his will, his DNA and our identity in him. **Worship** is key to experiencing intimacy with God. It is like touching the face of God. We hear him, experience him, and encounter him in ways that we do not normally. Healing occurs during worship. **Prayer.** Any relationship that we want to build, we must work on our communication. Talk to God as often as you think, about everything and anything. There is nothing that you cannot pray for and about.

One of the most important tools I learned in early recovery was the four absolutes of honesty, purity, unselfishness and love.[7] These are how we determine the difference between God's voice and our voice. Our voice is rooted in selfish, dishonest, fearful and resentful; basically, everything that was uncovered as a stronghold or defect in

---

[7] Dick B. *The Four Absolutes.* Silkworth.net.
http://silkworth.net/pages/aahistory/fourabsolutes1.php

the assessment conducted in movement 3. Pray and then spend time alone and quiet with the Lord. Then journal everything that comes into your mind. Now highlight all the thoughts that are in line with the four absolutes. Using this exercise helped me to start hearing from God. It was just the beginning of the journey of learning how to walk in the gifts of the spirit.

The gifts of the spirit.

"**4** There are different kinds of gifts, but the same Spirit distributes them.**5** There are different kinds of service, but the same Lord. **6** There are different kinds of working, but in all of them and in everyone it is the same God at work. **7** Now to each one the manifestation of the Spirit is given for the common good. **8** To one there is given through the Spirit a **message of wisdom**, to another a **message of knowledge** by means of the same Spirit, **9** to another **faith** by the same Spirit, to another gifts of **healing** by that one Spirit, **10** to another **miraculous powers**, to another **prophecy**, to another **distinguishing between spirits**, to another speaking in different kinds of **tongues**, and to still another the **interpretation of tongues**.**11** All these are the work of one and the same Spirit, and he distributes them to each one, just as he determines." (1 Cor 12:4-11 [NIV]).

There is so much literature and training on all these areas of spiritual growth, but the greatest experience that you will have is in spending time with the Holy Spirit and asking for guidance every day. As you minister to others in the 9th movement and walk through trials in life, God will manifest new aspects of himself through the gifts. We begin to understand what God's will is through allowing the Holy Spirit to lead us. When we practice this daily, it becomes natural to listen to God. (Romans 12:2 [NIV]). Going through the steps or these 9 movements is spiritual kindergarten that prepares us for the rest of the journey as disciples of Christ.

Take some to talk to God right now, then become very still and write down everything that comes into your mind. After you are done, highlight everything that is honesty, purity, unselfishness and love. Do you see the difference between God's voice and your own?

_____

_____

_____

_____

_____

_____

_____

_____

_____

_____

_____

_____

Now take some time to meditate on one verse: "For I can do all things through Christ who strengthens me" (Phil 4:13).

What are areas of your life, your desires and your passions that you do not believe this promise over your life? How can you allow God's power into that area of your life?

_____

_____

_____

_____

_____

_____

_____

What gifts of the spirit do you already know you have?

Take some time to pray and ask the Holy Spirit for the gifts that you would like to walk in.

9. We allow the Holy Spirit to operate through us, to fulfill our calling of making disciples of all nations and stay connected to the body of Christ.

Jesus delivered the Great Commission to his disciples to reach all nations for his namesake. This did not end with them, it extends to all believers. He assured them and assures us that he will be with us always.

> "Therefore go and make disciples of all nations, baptizing them in the name of the Father and of the Son and of the Holy Spirit, [20] and teaching them to obey everything I have commanded you. And **surely I am with you always**, to the very end of the age." (Matt 28:19-20 [NIV]).

Jesus entered the temple and proclaimed that he was the Messiah in front of the Pharisees. Although they had seen his many works, they still did not proclaim that he was the Messiah. He quoted an excerpt from Isaiah that was a prophecy of him coming long before he was even born.

> "The Spirit of the Sovereign Lord is on me, because **the Lord has anointed me to proclaim good news to the poor. He has sent me to bind up the brokenhearted, to proclaim freedom for the Captives and release from darkness for the prisoners,** [2] **to proclaim the year of the Lord's favor and the day of vengeance of our God, to comfort all who mourn,** [3] **and provide for those who grieve in Zion**—to bestow on them a crown of **beauty instead of ashes**, the **oil of joy instead of mourning**, and a **garment of praise** instead of a spirit of despair. They will be

called **oaks of righteousness**, a planting of the Lord **for the display of his splendor**." (Isaiah 61:1-3 [NIV]).

This same anointing is available to us as God's children and joint heirs to the throne. We are the Esther generation! Once you have experienced the broken feeling of walking in the flesh and the amazing restoration that occurs through the resurrection power of Christ; the only option is to tell the world and reach out to those around you, that are broken. The Holy Spirit will begin to operate in and through you in a way that is uniquely tailored to each person that you minister to. It is a beautiful experience to see the Holy Spirit open someone's heart and mind by ministering and sharing your own testimony. The more people that you minister to and mentor, the greater your intimacy with the Lord and the world around you. You will find purpose in him, in the identity that he has given you and the authority he has bestowed on you as his ambassador.

It is important to exercise wisdom when dealing with interventions of people who are addicted to substances. The first move is to send them to detox and **they must be willing**. The willingness is the hardest part. Only the Holy Spirit can bring people to a point of willingness. It is equally important to set healthy boundaries that allow the person to depend upon God and not on you. The risk of walking in codependence instead of the spirit is very high when ministering to others. We must always stay grounded in the spirit.

The resurrection power of Jesus is great enough to heal any affliction. We must truly believe that, often it is our faith that becomes the catalyst of healing others.

"'Nevertheless, I will bring health and healing to it; I will heal my people and will let them enjoy abundant peace and security." (Jeremiah 33:6 [NIV]).

"But he was pierced for our transgressions, he was crushed for our iniquities; the punishment that brought us peace was on him, and by his wounds we are healed." (Isaiah 53:5 [NIV]).

Jesus said that we would do even greater works (John 14:12 [NIV]). Let no circumstance overwhelm you, no matter how far someone has gone, God can reach them. Never let the enemy discourage, distract or deter you from stepping into your calling, there are people that need what you have to offer, Jesus.

"Jesus called his twelve disciples to him and gave them authority to drive out impure spirits and to heal every disease and sickness." (Matt 10:1 [NIV]).

"Heal the sick, raise the dead, cleanse those who have leprosy, drive out demons. Freely you have received; freely give." (Matt 10:8 [NIV]).

"Stretch out your hand to heal and perform signs and wonders through the name of your holy servant Jesus." (Acts 4:30 [NIV]).

One of my favorites stories in the bible is when the four men lowered the man down to be healed. (Luke 5:17-39 [NIV]). The inference is that when the men lowered the man down before Jesus to be healed, they had to let go of the ropes. This is the hardest part when dealing with the families of those that are struggling in the flesh. The Christian way is to always help those in need, but this story shows us that some people will not receive their healing until we let go. That does not mean to stop praying for them, this means to lay them at God's feet and intercede for them. It was the faith of his friends that brought this paralyzed man to Jesus. Many who are struggling in the flesh are paralyzed by the intense cycle that they are in and need intercession, but we cannot make them receive, they must take up their bed and walk. Once they decide to take this action, we can help them if we are teaching them to fish and not just dropping fish off at their door. They will grow much faster when they are relying upon God alone.

"For I am about to do something new. See, I have already begun! Do you not see it? I will make a pathway through the wilderness. I will create rivers in the dry wasteland." (Isaiah 43:19 [New Living Translation]). Sometimes it feels like a dream or vision is dead, but God always finishes the work that He begins. He will plant a dream or vision within us and once we align our vision with His, a pathway appears out of nowhere, provision comes flooding in, and illuminates the path.....it happens the moment we begin to MOVE FORWARD. Step out today and faith that He will make a way.

The Prophecies that Foretold and the Resurrection that Bears Witness that Christ is the One True God: An Essay for Those that Doubt

Introduction

Throughout history God continually sent his people messages in many ways to let them know that He was going to restore them into right relationship with Him. The entire Bible is a love story from God to humankind. The events of many lives were prophecies of Jesus coming and many of them through his own earthly lineage. The life of Jesus was a step-by-step fulfillment of Old Testament prophecy. The key piece and the grand finale is that of the resurrection of Christ. <u>Understanding the multitude of prophecies that point to Jesus coming and having legitimate proof of the resurrection are essential to prove that Christ is the one true God.</u>

Old Testament Prophecies that Pointed to the Messiah

The entire Old Testament is a storyline from the fall of man with Adam and Eve in the Garden of Eden when Eve ate the forbidden fruit and God prophesied, "And I will put enmity between you and the woman, and between your offspring and hers; he will crush your head, and you will strike his heal." (Genesis 3:15 [New International Version]). God is speaking to Satan saying that Eve's offspring,

Jesus would "crush" his "head" and that Satan would bruise his heal, the crucifixion. The remainder of the Old Testament is God sending prophet after prophet to foretell of the coming king, His son Jesus Christ to bridge the divide between man and God. The Bible is the greatest love story ever written and it is written to humanity from God.

Peter Dray discusses the essential differences of Christianity as opposed to other religions. The basis of which are historical facts and accounts of the prophesy of Christ tied to the actual events and occurrences that fulfill the same. Dray writes, "As you'll probably know, Christianity is a *historical* religion. <u>By this I mean that Christianity relies on certain events happening – if they didn't happen, then Christianity would completely unravel</u>." [8] The single most important factor to understand prior to studying the history of Old Testament prophecy is that the facts within the Bible have been historically and scientifically proven to be true, regardless of the many hands that have been involved in writing it.

---

[8] Dray, Peter. "'The Acts of the Risen Lord Jesus'." *Evangel* 26, no. 3 (September 2008): 66-71. *Academic Search Complete*, EBSCO*host* (accessed January 29, 2018). 1.

Jon Ruthven, discusses that although looking at Luke and Acts for fulfillment of prophecy are important; Isaiah, Hebrews, Jeremiah, and Ezekiel unlock a plethora of prophecy pointing to the Messiah.[9] Of these, Ruthven focuses on,

> "It appears that throughout the last five centuries of Christian scholarship, another equally explicit Old Testament promise of a covenant has been almost completely ignored, viz., Isa. 59.19-21. This passage, which also promises a new covenant, brought by the 'redeemer' upon repentance from sins is cited in the New Testament twice: Rom. 11.26-27 and Acts 2.38-39." [10]

Historical Reliability.

---

[9] Ruthven, Jon. "'This Is My Covenant with Them': Isaiah 59.19-21 as the Programmatic Prophecy of the New Covenant in the Acts of the Apostles (Part I)." *Journal of Pentecostal Theology* 17, no. 1 (October 2008): 32-47. *Academic Search Complete*, EBSCO*host* (accessed January 30, 2018). 2.

[10] Ruthven, Jon. "'This Is My Covenant with Them': Isaiah 59.19-21 as the Programmatic Prophecy of the New Covenant in the Acts of the Apostles (Part I)." *Journal of Pentecostal Theology* 17, no. 1 (October 2008): 32-47. *Academic Search Complete*, EBSCO*host* (accessed January 30, 2018). 1-17.

The greatest argument of unbelievers is the claim that the Bible is not accurate because it has been rewritten by too many people, particularly rewritten in the Dark Ages by the Roman Catholic Church. However, the Christian Broadcasting Network reports that hundreds of copies have been discovered by Archeologists that prove the historical accuracy of the written word.[11] The accuracy of the written word is what ties every testimony together, every prophecy and the resurrection. Every prophecy that was written was fulfilled in the life of Jesus and even the ancestors in his direct lineage.

Verses Foretelling of the Christ

The significance of the Old Testament prophecy testifying of the Messiah is so overwhelming to many, that it is not difficult to find several viewpoints of this analysis. For every prophecy in the Old Testament there is a fulfillment. For the purposes and length of this paper, the writer will focus on the key prophecies being foretold and fulfilled: that Jesus was born of a virgin, the way that He was

---

[11] Christian Broadcasting Network. "Biblical Prophecies Fulfilled by Jesus". CBN.com

http://www1.cbn.com/biblestudy/biblical-prophecies-fulfilled-by-jesus ¶7.

crucified, and the resurrection. These three are the outstanding supernatural manifestations that only God could perform.

Jesus was born of a virgin foretold.

The first prophecy that will be examined is that of Christ being born of a virgin. Never in history has a child been born of a virgin, nor since. This is a scientific impossibility and absolutely was at the time of the birth of Jesus. Isaiah, one of the major Old Testament Prophets, proclaimed, "Therefore, the Lord himself will give you a sign: The virgin will conceive and give birth to a son, and will call him Immanuel [God with us]." (Isaiah 7:14 [NIV]). The next verse that is provided by the Christian Broadcasting Network is,

> "For to us a child is born, to us a son is given, and the government will be on his shoulders. And he will be called Wonderful Counselor, Mighty God, Everlasting Father, Prince of Peace. Of the greatness of his government and peace there will be no end. He will reign on David's throne and over his kingdom, establishing and upholding it with justice and righteousness from that time on and forever. The zeal of the Lord Almighty will accomplish this." (Isaiah 9:6-7 [NIV]). [12]

---

[12] Christian Broadcasting Network. "Biblical Prophecies Fulfilled by Jesus". CBN.com

http://www1.cbn.com/biblestudy/biblical-prophecies-fulfilled-by-jesus ¶ 18-19.

The significance of these two prophecies about the Messiah, indicate that his existence would be supernaturally manifested by God to rule and reign over all the kingdoms of heaven and earth. "Immanuel" means "God with us" and indicates that the Messiah is God in the human form.

The way Jesus was Crucified foretold.

The way that Jesus was crucified parallels the religious rituals at the time, of offering sacrifice to maintain right relationship with God. In religious sacrifice, the animal's bones could not be broken (Numbers 9:12 [NIV]), yet in crucifixion the legs had to be broken to ensure complete expiration. Jesus Christ is the only crucifixion that the legs were not broken (John 19:31-36 [NIV]).[13] This was prophesied by David, "he protects all his bones, not one of them will be broken." (Psalm 34:20 [NIV]). Hundreds of years before the birth of Jesus, Isaiah prophesied, "But He was wounded for our transgressions, He was bruised for our iniquities; The chastisement for our peace was upon Him, And by His stripes we are

---

[13] Bible Probe. "365 Messianic Prophecies". BibleProbe.com

https://www.bibleprobe.com/365messianicprophecies.htm

healed." (Isaiah 53:5 [NIV]). This is the foretelling of the Messiah as our savior, that through his crucifixion, or sacrifice, we would be healed or saved for all eternity. This sacrifice would eternally bridge the divide between God and man.

Jesus' resurrection from the dead foretold

The resurrection is the key prophecy that differentiates Jesus as Lord from any other who has claimed to be one that is sent with divine revelation. There are numerous prophecies that indicate the resurrection would occur, but more important the lives of the lineage of Christ himself all foretold of His coming to annihilate the enemy, Satan. <u>The story of Rahab, Boaz and Ruth, and David</u> are all prophecies indicating that Jesus would come and save his people. Rahab, in the book of Joshua, is a prostitute; obviously, a sinner, whose faith in God saved her entire family, just like Jesus saved the entire human race (Joshua [NIV]). <u>The story of Ruth and Boaz is another prophecy</u> of how God would restore all that was lost in the fall of man, just like he restored all that Ruth had lost (Ruth [NIV<u>]).</u> <u>The story of David and Goliath,</u> David is the underdog, just like humanity is, in our fallen and sinful nature. David, the smallest of all his brothers, is chosen by God to defeat the Philistine giant, Goliath (the enemy). He fights in the name of the Lord and vindicates his people the Israelites. (1 Samuel 17 [NIV]). The most amazing part of this story is that he cuts off the giant's head and takes it to the same hill (Calvary or Golgotha, meaning the "place of the skull") that his descendent, Jesus Christ, would one day be crucified to vindicate His people.

Fulfillment of the Prophecies in the life of Jesus

Dray uses Luke and the book of Acts to display the numerous accounts of promises (prophesy) fulfilled. Dray specifically focuses on Luke 24:26-27 recounting the words of Jesus, "Did not the Christ have to suffer these things and then enter his glory? And beginning with Moses and all the Prophets, he explained to them what was said in all the Scriptures concerning himself." [14]

<u>Israel Knohl, analyzes the published work of Ada Yardeni and Binyamin Elitzur that entails a complete analysis of the</u>

---

[14] Dray, Peter. "'The Acts of the Risen Lord Jesus'." *Evangel* 26, no. 3 (September 2008): 66-71. *Academic Search Complete*, EBSCO*host* (accessed January 29, 2018). 1.

translation of the *Hazon Gabriel*. *Hazon Gabriel* is referred to as a transmission by the angel Gabriel.[15] The entire translation is fascinating and parallels all the prophesy woven through the Old Testament concerning the Messiah. The two most prominent translations that Israel Knohl opens the article with are,

"By three days you shall know that, thus said the Lord of Hosts, the God of Israel, the evil has broken by righteousness…. In just a little while, I will shake the heavens and the earth."[16] This is obviously a prophecy given before the crucifixion of Jesus foretelling of the same and the resurrection to follow. The interesting part is that most people thought that Jesus would be a leader that would free them from political oppression, however, He was coming to free them from the spiritual oppression from the enemy, Satan. The intricate and beautiful translations continue to reveal the spiritual nature and significance of the "Messiah son of Joseph".

---

[15] Knohl, Israel. "By Three Days, Live": Messiahs, Resurrection, and Ascent to Heaven in Hazon Gabriel." *Journal of Religion* 88, no. 2 (April 2008): 147-158. *Academic Search Complete*, EBSCO*host* (accessed January 29, 2018). 1.

[16] Knohl, Israel. "By Three Days, Live": Messiahs, Resurrection, and Ascent to Heaven in Hazon Gabriel." *Journal of Religion* 88, no. 2 (April 2008): 147-158. *Academic Search Complete*, EBSCO*host* (accessed January 29, 2018). 1.

Jesus was born of a virgin fulfilled.

The fulfillment of the prophecies in Isaiah about the Messiah that would come supernaturally to rule over the heavens and earth for eternity is shown in the virgin birth of Jesus. **The major question is: how do we know that this happened**? God did not just tell one person, Mary, by visiting her with an angel (Luke 1:26-38 [NIV]). This would have caused uproar. He sent an angel to Joseph (Matt 1:20-23 [NIV]), then to wise men (Matt 2:1-2 [NIV]), then to random shepherds (Luke 2:8-20 [NIV]). There were four different visitations and revelations that Jesus was the Messiah. The remainder of His life, death and resurrection were proof of the same.

The way Jesus was Crucified fulfilled.

David Norman discusses the essential components of belief in the death and the resurrection as true and factual for full understanding and belief in Christ as the one true God. He produces an in-depth analysis of the historical accounts of those that witnessed the risen Lord. He endeavors to view the perception of the witnesses based on the societal norms of the time.

> "Doubt plays a major role in the empty tomb and resurrection appearance accounts. My thesis is that doubt finds its resolution more in the "why" of faith, than in the "what." The

second part of my article focuses on the postburial accounts of the four Gospels. I argue that there can be no faith in the resurrection/exaltation of Jesus that does not address the stumbling block to faith caused by Jesus' death and burial. Accepting Jesus' death is as important as acknowledging his resurrection from the dead." [17]

Particularly of importance was the fact that Jesus asked the disciples to touch his wounds. It is at this point that even Thomas finally believed.

The prophecies about the crucifixion in Numbers, Psalms and Isaiah all foretold of the gruesome crucifixion. The piercing of the hands and feet, being betrayed by His own people, the lashings and beatings. However, the most unique and gripping portion of this event is that out of all those crucified that day, Jesus Christ was the only one that the soldiers did not break the legs.

> "Now it was the day of Preparation, and the next day was to be a special Sabbath. Because the Jewish leaders did not want the bodies left on the crosses during the Sabbath, they asked Pilate to have the legs broken and the bodies taken down. 32 The soldiers therefore came and broke the legs of the first man who had been crucified with Jesus, and then those of the other. 33 But when they came to Jesus and found that he was already dead, **they did not break his legs.** 34 Instead, one of the soldiers **pierced Jesus' side with a spear,**

---

[17] Norman, David J. 2008. "DOUBT AND THE RESURRECTION OF JESUS." *Theological Studies* 69, no. 4: 786-811. *Academic Search Complete*, EBSCO*host* (accessed January 26, 2018). 2.

bringing a sudden flow of blood and water. 35 The man who saw it has given testimony, and his testimony is true. He knows that he tells the truth, and he testifies so that you also may believe. 36 **These things happened so that the scripture would be fulfilled: "Not one of his bones will be broken,"** (John 19:31-36 [NIV]).

He became the perfect sacrifice for us. He was without sin and everything down to the way that he was crucified fell in line with God's Old Testament law, breaking the power of the sin, death and the law. "God made him who had no sin to be sin for us, so that in him we might become the righteousness of God." (2 Cor 5:21 [NIV]).

Jesus' resurrection from the dead fulfilled.

Jesus appeared first to Mary Magdalene (John 20:14-16 [NIV]). Then an angel appeared to "Mary the Mother of James, Salome, and Joanna telling them that Jesus had risen, "Suddenly Jesus met them. "Greetings," he said. They came to him, clasped his feet and worshipped him." (Matthew 28:9 [NIV]). [18] If that was not enough, he then appeared to Peter (Luke 24:34 [NIV]). Don Stewart continues to present the accounts that occurred on Easter Sunday

---

[18] Stewart, Don. "To Whom Did Jesus Appear after His Death?" BlueLetterBible.org

https://www.blueletterbible.org/faq/don_stewart/don_stewart_814.cfm

directly from the word, "two disciples on the Emmaus Road [(Luke 24:13-16 [NIV])]…the disciples [(John 20:19,20,24 [NIV])]…all of the disciples [(John 20:26-28 [NIV])]…a mountain in Galilee [(Matthew 28:16,17 [NIV])]….over five hundred people [(1 Cor 15:6 [NIV])]." [19] The list goes on and on. God knows the inquisitive nature of humankind, our deepest desire is to question that which exists, as evidenced by our decision in the Garden of Eden. He knew that we would need thousands of years of proof to believe that Jesus was truly God and man, that he was born of a virgin, that he died by crucifixion, to be a sacrifice for humanity, and that he resurrected from the grips of death.

Conclusion

Numerous points have been displayed that lay tribute to the countless prophecies that God supernaturally sent through His people throughout the Old Testament. He has woven His truth throughout history, through the lives of his people, but most

---

[19] Stewart, Don. "To Whom Did Jesus Appear after His Death?" BlueLetterBible.org

https://www.blueletterbible.org/faq/don_stewart/don_stewart_814.cfm

importantly through His son, Jesus. Jesus's life was a testament and fulfillment of the promises of God. Understanding the multitude of prophecies that point to Jesus coming and having legitimate proof of the resurrection are essential to prove that Christ is the one true God, three in one: Father, Son and Holy Spirit. These are essential facts that any Christian should be ready to witness to.

Bibliography

Alcoholics Anonymous World Services, Inc., *Alcoholics Anonymous*. New York City: The AA Grapevine, 2001. http://research.easybib.com/research/index/search?search=%22Alcoholics+Anonymous%22&&sort_by=rank&medium=on_line&filters%5Bdatasource%5D=easybib

Bible Probe. "365 Messianic Prophecies". BibleProbe.com https://www.bibleprobe.com/365messianicprophecies.htm

Bible Study Tools. Revive; Reviving. Biblestudytools.com https://www.biblestudytools.com/dictionary/revive-reviving/

Christian Broadcasting Network. "Biblical Prophecies Fulfilled by Jesus". CBN.com http://www1.cbn.com/biblestudy/biblical-prophecies-fulfilled-by-jesus

Coogan, Michael. *Oxford Biblical Studies Online*. Oxford, United Kingdom: Oxford University Press USA., 2009.

Dick B. *The Four Absolutes*. Silkworth.net. http://silkworth.net/pages/aahistory/fourabsolutes1.php

Dray, Peter. "'The Acts of the Risen Lord Jesus'." *Evangel* 26, no. 3 (September 2008): 66-71. *Academic Search Complete*, EBSCO*host* (accessed January 29, 2018).

Elwell, Walter, A. *Bakers Evangelical Dictionary of Biblical Theology*. Grand Rapids, MI: Baker Books, 1996. (accessed November 5, 2015 from http://www.studylight.org/dictionaries/bed/view.cgi?n=300).

Father Heart Communications. *The Fathers Love Letter*. FathersLoveLetter.com http://www.fathersloveletter.com/text.html

Gaebelein, A.C. The Work of Christ: Past, Present and Future. Publication Office "Our Hope". Accessed January 30, 2018. GCU Library.

Hengstenberg, Ernst. *Christiology of the Old Testament: And a Commentary on the Messianic Predictions. Vol.2*, Grand Rapids, Michigan: Kregel Publications, 1956.

Investopedia. Mututally Exclusive. Investopedia.com https://www.investopedia.com/terms/m/mutuallyexclusive.asp

Jews for Jesus. "Top 40 Most Helpful Messianic Prophecies". Jewsforjesus.org https://jewsforjesus.org/answers/top-40-most-helpful-messianic-prophecies/

Knohl, Israel. "By Three Days, Live": Messiahs, Resurrection, and Ascent to Heaven in Hazon Gabriel." *Journal of Religion* 88, no. 2 (April 2008): 147-158. *Academic Search Complete*, EBSCO*host* (accessed January 29, 2018).

MacArthur, John. *The MacArthur Bible Commentary*. Nashville, TN: Thomas Nelson Inc., 2005.

Miller, Robert J. 2015. Helping Jesus Fulfill Prophecy. Eugene: Wipf and Stock Publishers. Accessed January 29, 2018. ProQuest Ebook Central.

Norman, David J. 2008. "DOUBT AND THE RESURRECTION OF JESUS." *Theological Studies* 69, no. 4: 786-811. *Academic Search Complete*, EBSCO*host* (accessed January 26, 2018).

Overeaters Anonymous. *Step Four Resentments Checklist Column 4.* Oapalmbeachfl.org http://oapalmbeachfl.org/documents/Step4_Inventory_Sheets.pdf

Ruthven, Jon. "'This Is My Covenant with Them': Isaiah 59.19-21 as the Programmatic Prophecy of the New Covenant in the Acts of the Apostles (Part I)." *Journal of Pentecostal Theology* 17, no. 1 (October 2008): 32-47. *Academic Search Complete*, EBSCO*host* (accessed January 30, 2018).

Ruthven, Jon. "'This is My Covenant with Them': Isaiah 59.19-21 as the Programmatic Prophecy of the New Covenant in the Acts of the Apostles (Part II)." *Journal of Pentecostal Theology* 17, no. 2 (April 2009): 219-237. *Academic Search Complete*, EBSCO*host* (accessed January 30, 2018).

St. Mary Parish. "The Robe, The Ring and The Sandals." Smpgilroy.org http://smpgilroy.org/multimedia-archive/september-11-2016/

Stewart, Don. "To Whom Did Jesus Appear after His Death?" BlueLetterBible.org https://www.blueletterbible.org/faq/don_stewart/don_stewart_814.cfm

The Bible Study Site. Meaning of Numbers in the Bible the Number 9. Biblestudy.org http://www.biblestudy.org/bibleref/meaning-of-numbers-in-bible/9.html

Thom, G. "JESUS AND "THE DANIEL CODE.." *Acta Theologica* 31, no. 2 (June 2011): 278-294. *Academic Search Complete*, EBSCO*host* (accessed January 30, 2018).

Warren, Rick. "More Than 300 Biblical Prophecies Point to Jesus". Pastorrick.com http://pastorrick.com/devotional/english/full-post/more-than-300-biblical-prophecies-point-to-jesus1

Made in the USA
Columbia, SC
11 June 2025